Dinosaur Detectives
Search for the facts...

Tyrannosaurus
and Other
Cretaceous Dinosaurs

Tracey Kelly

raintree
a Capstone company — publishers for children

Raintree is an imprint of Capstone Global Library Limited, a company incorporated in England and Wales having its registered office at 264 Banbury Road, Oxford, OX2 7DY – Registered company number: 6695582

www.raintree.co.uk
myorders@raintree.co.uk

Text: Tracey Kelly
Designer: John Woolford
Design Manager: Keith Davis
Editorial Director: Lindsey Lowe
Children's Publisher: Anne O'Daly
Picture Manager: Sophie Mortimer
Production by Katie LaVigne
Printed and bound in India

ISBN 978 1 4747 7832 9 (hardback)
ISBN 978 1 4747 7838 1 (paperback)

British Library Cataloguing in Publication Data
A full catalogue record for this book is available from the British Library.

Acknowledgements
We would like to thank the following for permission to reproduce photographs:
Public Domain: Connie Ma 4.

Every effort has been made to contact copyright holders of material reproduced in this book. Any omissions will be rectified in subsequent printings if notice is given to the publisher.

All the internet addresses (URLs) given in this book were valid at the time of going to press. However, due to the dynamic nature of the internet, some addresses may have changed, or sites may have changed or ceased to exist since publication. While the author and publisher regret any inconvenience this may cause readers, no responsibility for any such changes can be accepted by either the author or the publisher.

Contents

How do we know about dinosaurs?

Scientists are like detectives.

They look at dinosaur fossils.

Fossils tell us where dinosaurs lived.

They tell us how big they were.

This *Tyrannosaurus* skeleton is named Sue. She is 67 million years old! Sue is the largest *Tyrannosaurus* ever found. She is 12 metres (40 feet) long.

How to use this book

This tells you what the animal ate.

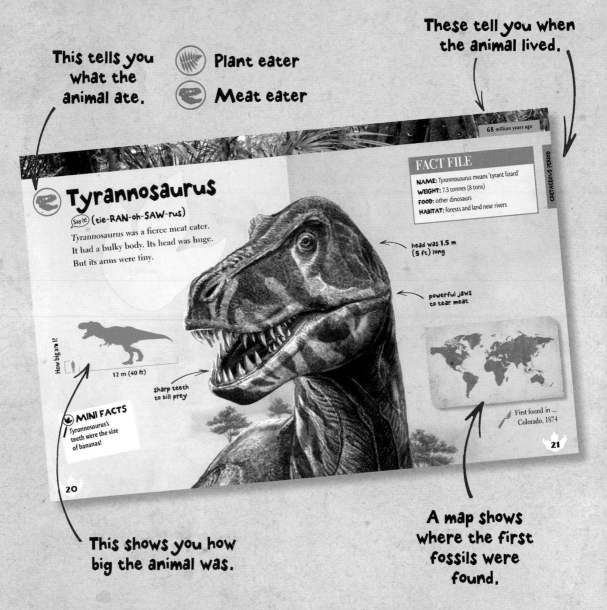

Plant eater

Meat eater

These tell you when the animal lived.

68 million years ago

CRETACEOUS PERIOD

Tyrannosaurus

(Say it!) (tie-RAN-oh-SAW-rus)

Tyrannosaurus was a fierce meat eater. It had a bulky body. Its head was huge. But its arms were tiny.

FACT FILE

NAME: Tyrannosaurus means 'tyrant lizard'
WEIGHT: 7.3 tonnes (8 tons)
FOOD: other dinosaurs
HABITAT: forests and land near rivers

head was 1.5 m (5 ft) long

powerful jaws to tear meat

How big am I?

12 m (40 ft)

sharp teeth to kill prey

MINI FACTS
Tyrannosaurus's teeth were the size of bananas!

First found in ... Colorado, 1874

20

21

This shows you how big the animal was.

A map shows where the first fossils were found.

Read on to become a dinosaur detective!

What was Earth like?

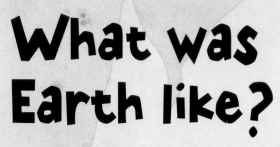

Tyrannosaurus lived in the Cretaceous period. That was more than 65 million years ago. The land was dry but many rivers flowed through it. They were full of fish. Plants grew near the water.

Argentinosaurus

(Say it!) (AR-jen-TEEN-oh-SAW-rus)

Argentinosaurus was a giant plant eater.
It had a long neck! It ate tonnes of food
every day. It plodded along slowly on four
huge legs.

How big am I?

30 m (100 ft.)

long tail to
balance big body

 **MINI FACTS**

Argentinosaurus
lived in herds.
The young were
in the middle.
That kept them safe.

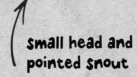

small head and
pointed snout

long neck
and back

FACT FILE

NAME: *Argentinosaurus* means
'Argentine lizard'

WEIGHT: 50–100 tonnes
(55–110 tons)

FOOD: plants and tree leaves

HABITAT: evergreen forests

First found in ...
Argentina, 1987

Baryonyx

Say it! **(BAR-ee-ON-icks)**

Baryonyx was a meat eater. It ate fish too! It caught them with its sharp claws.

patterned skin

⬤ MINI FACTS
Baryonyx's claws were 35 centimetres (12 inches) long!

stiff tail

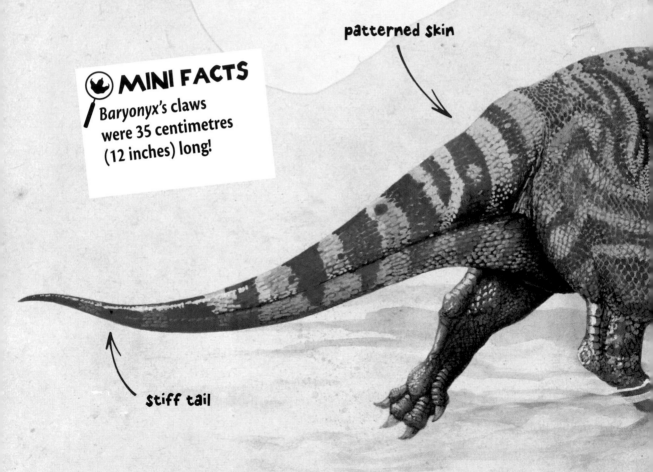

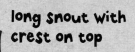

long snout with crest on top

FACT FILE

NAME: *Baryonyx* means 'heavy claw'

WEIGHT: 1.4–2.0 tonnes (1.5–2.2 tons)

FOOD: fish and meat

HABITAT: forests and meadows around rivers, lakes and swamps

How big am I?

10 m (33 ft.)

sharp claws to hook fish

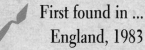

First found in ...
England, 1983

11

Gallimimus

Say it! **(GAL-ee-MEE-mus)**

Gallimimus looked like an ostrich.
But it had a tail! It lived in small herds.
It could see very well.

eyes looked
sideways to
spot danger

long, stiff tail

MINI FACTS

Gallimimus could run
up to 69 kilometres
(43 miles) per hour.
That's as fast as a car!

long back legs

12

FACT FILE

NAME: *Gallimimus* means 'chicken mimic'

WEIGHT: 440 kg (970 lbs.)

FOOD: small animals, insects, plants and eggs

HABITAT: near rivers, streams and shallow lakes

How big am I?

6 m (20 ft.)

sharp claws

First found in ...
Mongolia, 1963

13

Iguanodon

Say it! (ig-WAH-no-don)

Iguanodon was a plant eater.
It grabbed plants with its beak.
Iguanodon had big thumb spikes.
It could stab other dinosaurs!

How big am I?

10 m (33 ft.)

strong tail
to balance
heavy body

MINI FACTS

Iguanodon was the
second dinosaur
to be named.

FACT FILE

NAME: *Iguanodon* means 'iguana tooth'

WEIGHT: about 3 tonnes (3.5 tons)

FOOD: plants

HABITAT: swampy places, plains, forests, mountains, deserts and beaches

thick neck

thumb spikes

strong legs

First found in ...
England, 1822

15

Oviraptor

Say it! **(OH-vih-RAP-tor)**

Oviraptor was as fast as an ostrich!
It had three fingers on each hand.
Oviraptor had a powerful beak.
It could crack open hard food.

How big am I?

2 m (6.5 ft.)

wavy tail to balance body

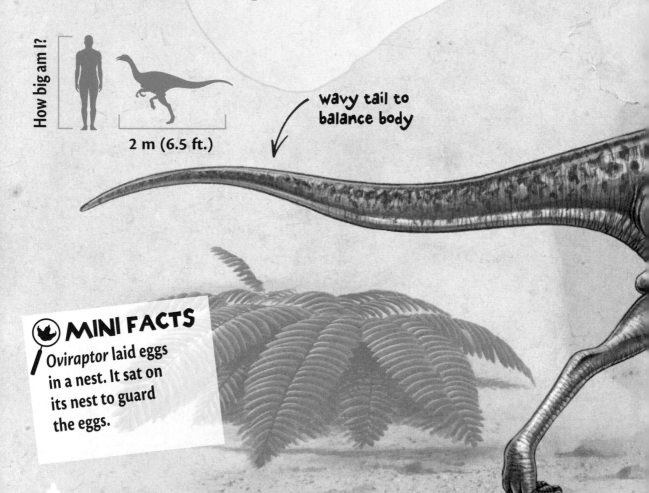

🔍 MINI FACTS

Oviraptor laid eggs in a nest. It sat on its nest to guard the eggs.

FACT FILE

NAME: *Oviraptor* means 'egg hunter'
WEIGHT: 35 kg (77 lbs.)
FOOD: hard fruits, nuts, eggs and possibly shellfish
HABITAT: deserts and dry areas

heavy body

horny beak

hands with
three fingers
and claws

First found in ...
Mongolia, 1923

Triceratops

Say it! (try-SER-ah-TOPS)

Triceratops was a massive plant eater. Its head had three horns. It had a bony neck frill. *Triceratops* lived in North America.

🔍 **MINI FACTS**

Triceratops had 400 to 800 teeth! It only used a few at a time.

young and old walked in herds

powerful legs

FACT FILE

NAME: *Triceratops* means 'three-horned face'
WEIGHT: 5.4 tonnes (6 tons)
FOOD: twigs and leaves
HABITAT: open woodlands

bony neck frill

two long horns
for fighting

How big am I?

9 m (30 ft.)

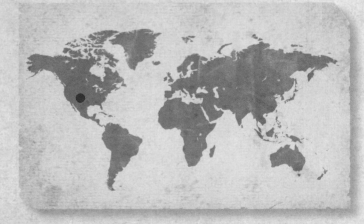

First found in ...
Colorado, United States, 1887

strong toes

19

Tyrannosaurus

Say it! (tie-RAN-oh-SAW-rus)

Tyrannosaurus was a fierce meat eater.
It had a bulky body. Its head was huge.
But its arms were tiny.

How big am I?

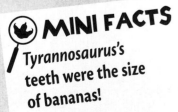

12 m (40 ft.)

sharp teeth
to kill prey

MINI FACTS

Tyrannosaurus's
teeth were the size
of bananas!

FACT FILE

NAME: *Tyrannosaurus* means 'tyrant lizard'

WEIGHT: 7.3 tonnes (8 tons)

FOOD: other dinosaurs

HABITAT: forests and land near rivers

head was 1.5 m
(5 ft.) long

powerful jaws
to tear meat

First found in ...
Colorado, United States, 1874

Dinosaur quiz

Test your dinosaur detective skills! Can you answer these questions? Look in the book for clues. The answers are on page 24.

2 Which dinosaur looked like an ostrich with a tail?

1 Which dinosaur caught fish?

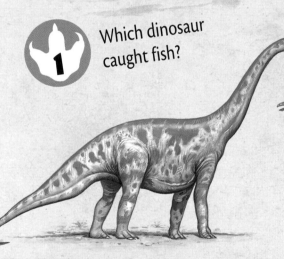

3 Which dinosaur ate tonnes of food every day?

4 How did *Oviraptor* make its young?

22

Glossary

fossil
Part of an animal or plant in rock.
The animal or plant lived in ancient times.

habitat
The kind of place where an animal
usually lives.

herd
A group of animals
that lives together.

meat eater
An animal that eats
mostly meat.

plant eater
An animal that eats only
plants, not meat.

Find out more

Books

Dinosaurs (Collins Fascinating Facts),
Collins Editors (Collins, 2016)

The Big Book of Dinosaurs,
DK Editors (DK Children, 2015)

Websites

www.dinosaurpictures.org/
cretaceous-dinosaurs

www.dkfindout.com/uk/dinosaurs-
and-prehistoric-life

www.nhm.ac.uk/discover/dino-
directory

Index

Quiz answers: 1. *Baryonyx* caught fish with its sharp claws. **2.** *Gallimimus* looked like an ostrich. **3.** *Argentinosaurus* ate tonnes of food every day. **4.** *Oviraptor* laid eggs in a nest and sat on them.